THE GEORGE V
Four Seasons of Pleasure

FOUR

Graphic Design: Élisabeth Welter

Editing Coordination: Julie Houis

Visit www.lamartiniere.fr

THE GEORGE V
Four Seasons of Pleasure

Written by André Bercoff

FOUR SEASONS HOTEL
George V
Paris

Éditions
de La Martinière

Go up along the Seine. The Seine, flowing through Paris, its presence gliding through the soul of the city, emanating its pervasive calm... and our loves, must we remember them? as the poet said. There it is. At the heart of the "golden triangle," marked out for the ages by the Alma Bridge and the Eiffel Tower, the Place de la Concorde with the Obelisk, and the Place de l'Étoile (or Place Charles de Gaulle) with its Arc de Triomphe; here is where one of the world's most resplendent palace hotels has stood for seventy years. On foot, by horseback or by boat, all roads lead to the George V. Those who enter here are also stepping into the legend of Paris.

Everyone has their own favorite take on France's capital. Some sing the praises of Saint-Germain-des-Prés, with its lively ferment of culture and ideas, verbal insurrections, or barricades that were strategically placed here. Others wax nostalgic over Montmartre as it was a hundred years ago, with its *moulins*, its *galettes*, its painters and ruffians. And there are those who still yearn for the Bohemian atmosphere of Montparnasse in the 1930s. Not to mention those who are partial to the Bastille and the dance halls on the Rue de Lappe, the novelists on the *fortifs*, or border zone, or the fog on the Tolbiac Bridge, or those who will always remember the belly of Paris when the Halles quarter was still filled with a slaughterhouse. But who can deny that the most luxurious part of Paris, where its secret aristocracy has lived for ages, is between the shimmering necklace made up of the Champs-Élysées, Avenue Montaigne and Avenue George V and the Alma Bridge.

Right from the start, let's seek out the magic of this place. Three centuries ago, this was still a wooded area. Yes, right here along the Champs-Élysées, there was still an unnamed swampy prairie.

"It used to be a plain that you could see to the right of Cours la Reine, which you could reach by crossing a small stone bridge. In 1670, it was planted with elms that formed handsome alleys all the way to Roule, and ended in a star formation, right at the point where you could see a part of the city and the surrounding countryside, which was known as the Champs-Élysées. The main alley was more spacious than the rest, and ended on one side in a large esplanade facing

the swing bridge at the Tuileries, which has since become the Place de Louis XV [and is now the Place de la Concorde], and at the other end, the Étoile [which means star]."

Thus was it described by Hurtaut and Magny, in their *Dictionnaire historique de la Ville de Paris et de ses environs,* in the year of our Lord 1779. In his magnificent book called *L'Invention de Paris,* Eric Hazan recalls that at the end of the 18th century, the Champs-Élysées was crammed with terraced houses, immense cafés, fashion and jewelry shops and a variety of sparkling shows, masked balls and fireworks. Patrons dined at the Ledoyen, built in 1800 – the only restaurant in the environs at the time – or frequented the Café des Ambassadeurs and the lavish hotel commissioned by Grimod de La Reynière – which currently houses the United States Embassy.

Here is how Chateaubriand described the quarter around the Champs-Élysées in 1800: "On entering the Champs-Elysées I was amazed to hear the sounds of violins, horns, clarinets and drums. I saw dance-halls where men and women were dancing; further on, the Tuileries palace appeared at the far end of its two great stands of chestnut trees. As for the Place Louis XV, it was bare; it had the ruined look, melancholy and deserted, of an ancient amphitheatre; I passed it swiftly; I was quite surprised not to hear any groans; I was fearful of putting my foot in a pool of blood of which there was not a trace; my eyes were drawn to that corner of sky where the instrument of death had towered; I thought I could see my brother and sister-in-law in their shifts lying beneath the blood-drenched machine: there Louis XVI's head fell. Despite the joyful streets, the church towers were silent; it felt as though I was returning on that day of immense grief, Good Friday." *(Memoirs from beyond the tomb – as translated by A.S. Kline)*

After that point, however, the legend of the Champs-Élysées just continued to grow more beautiful. In 1858, Victor Fournel celebrated this quarter that was "the center of that deluge of harmony that overflows in Paris during the warm months. You can barely take a step, from the Rond-Point to Concorde, without getting blasted right in the chest, like a burst of artillery, with a ballad here, a ditty there, a bit further, an aria or the overture of an opera." It was on one of the broad avenues of the golden triangle, the Avenue Montaigne, formerly called the

Allée des Veuves, that in 1844 the Mabille brothers opened a dance hall that attracted all the high society of Paris. In the gardens on the Champs-Élysées there was a flourishing of the greatest music-hall cafés, the Alcazar and the Café des Ambassadeurs, where such immortal painters as Degas and Toulouse-Lautrec would paint some of their most famous portraits. Nowadays, the only establishment on the Champs-Élysées that evokes and symbolizes the splendor of the past is the Lido, where foreigners, provincials and Parisians come to celebrate the fact that "Paris will always be Paris" 365 days a year.

Of course, it was not until the 20th century that the Champs-Élysées truly began to sparkle with all of its glory. How could we forget about Le Fouquet's, at the corner of the Champs-Élysées and the Avenue George V, which was founded in 1901 and quickly became the favored meeting place for all the horse owners, racegoers and beautiful women who frequented the race courses at Longchamp, Deauville and elsewhere. Our Paris wanderer, Léon-Paul Fargue, wrote in *Le Piéton de Paris*, "Le Fouquet's is one of those places that will only go out of style if it gets bombed. And even then! Other cafés dwindle, lose their patrons, close and go bankrupt. Le Fouquet's keeps going, like a vital organ. It is a place for male gossip – because men gossip just as much as women." Later, between the world wars, Le Fouquet's would become what it still is today: a meeting place for movie and audiovisual people, from Raimu to Lino Ventura,

Gabin, Belmondo, Arletty and Jean Reno, as well as many others. There is no César awards evening that does not end with a fine dinner at this famous gastronomic landmark. Moreover, if you wanted to see a movie in the original version in Paris, there was a long time when you could only find them at the Marignan, Normandie or Colisée movie theaters. The Champs-Élysées is a veritable history book. Each year, the Bastille Day parade on July 14th consecrates the French nation. And when *Les Bleus* – the French soccer team – wins the World Cup, hundreds of thousands of admirers gather here to celebrate until dawn.

And you cannot pass a certain gallery on the Champs without evoking the Claridge, a renowned hotel that has since been transformed into an apartment building, inhabited, like the George V, by numerous stars. Just take a stroll down the immense avenue, along its vast sidewalks, starting at the Étoile, to contemplate the specter of the Astoria hotel, replaced half a century ago by the Publicis building with a glass façade, which then burned down and was rebuilt. A few dozen meters further down, you'll see the Élysée Palace, another famous hotel built in 1897 that now houses the headquarters of a bank, but whose *Style Nouille* and *rococo* façade has remained unchanged. Further down again, on the same sidewalk, the Païva hotel built in 1855. It has since been transformed into a private club, but still features one of the rare façades reminiscent of the luxurious Belle Époque. We soon come to the Grand Palais, built between 1897 and 1900, which housed the Universal Expo in that year. Twenty-five years later, the International Exhibition of Decorative Arts saw the explosion of the *Art Déco* and *Art Nouveau* styles, which prevailed during the construction in 1928 of a certain Hotel George V. The façade of this palace has since been classified as a historical monument.

As you leave the George V, you can also head in the opposite direction, towards the Place de l'Alma, to go and enjoy a *steak tartare* on the terrace at Chez Francis, the famous restaurant founded in 1919 that inspired Jean Giraudoux for the décor in the first act of *La Folle de Chaillot*. There are certain fall afternoons along the Seine when, despite the heavy traffic, you can almost imagine the presence of Marguerite Monod.

ENTENTE CORDIALE

Two professionals were in charge of the actual work of resurrecting the Hotel George V in the year 2000. Architect Richard Martinet renovated the buildings' façades and exteriors, redrawing each window, balcony and room of the hotel from the original plans and drawings of the 1920s. Pierre-Yves Rochon, devoted his talents to the decoration of both the public and private areas, from guest room to suite, and restaurant to salon. The rooms, which average between 35 and 50 sq. m. in size, feature a characteristic luminosity that is soft and bright at the same time, a harmony of light, soothing colors, comfort and technological equipment that meets the highest standards. The central, unifying idea was that this hotel should, by virtue of its shapes and tones, lines and tints, belong to a purely French heritage, enhanced with a British touch. The atmosphere is dominated by beige, gray and off-white fabrics, paint and marble, as well as harmonies of straw yellow and gold, sky blue and sapphire, sea green and emerald, in the Lyon silks and damasks. Marquetry commodes and Boulle furnishings round out the personality of the whole.

At the Hotel George V, the very identity of the establishment marks everything with the stamp of the *Entente Cordiale* and Franco-British aesthetics.

BELOW AND OPPOSITE The *Le Cinq* restaurant,
Bar and Lobby. Drawings for the George V's complete
renovation by interior designer Pierre-Yves Rochon, 1997.

PRECEDING PAGE The Gallery.

OPPOSITE Mantle clock dating back to the beginning
of the 18th century.

BELOW Decorative details.

LE PRINTEMPS

YE WHO
ENTER HERE....

...contemplate the visible signs of *Entente Cordiale* with admiration. On the floor, lustrous marble in yellow Sienna, gray and beige. At the center, a Regency display table in mahogany is surrounded by armchairs in the Empire spirit, covered in a golden embossed pile fabric. Behind the concierge's desk reigns the magnificent tapestry, Allegory of War and Peace, dating from the end of the reign of Louis XIV and a part of the outstanding collection of antiques belonging to the George V, constituted in the 1930s by Mr. and Mrs. François Dupré. The crystal and bronze chandelier, 2.20 m. high and 1.60 in diameter, was made partially in Florence. On the wall behind the reception desk hangs a copy of the famous painting by Nicolas Poussin called "Landscape with Diogenes". The two consoles in the reception and concierge's office date from the 19th century, while those standing near the boutique are inspired by the Russian style. The bronzes are originals and the four white marble statues embody the four seasons, which are a natural emblem for a hotel that operates 24 hours a day, 365 days a year. The natural light, which enters from the open-air marble court and the openings in the façade, is complemented by diffused artificial lighting. In this place, everything is planned to welcome guests in a warm, gentle and calm atmosphere.

A WHIFF OF
THE COUNTRY

From the origins of the George V, the Marble
Court has always been the hotel's park: a patio
under the open sky that is transformed, from the
first days of spring, into a leafy arbor with flowers, where visitors and diners may enjoy a heady
day in the country, just a few steps from the
Champs-Élysées.

The Gallery runs the length of one side of the
Marble Court. On the inside, Louis XV and
Louis XVI furnishings, Regency armchairs and
English pedestal tables and consoles harmonize
well, under the shadow of a pianist that no one
would ever dream of shooting. The splendid
Savonnerie rug from the Aubusson factory was
fully restored during the renovations of the Four
Seasons Hotel George V. The two Flanders tapestries that complete the décor provide a perfect
accord of blues, yellows, greens and reds. One of
them, from the Leyniers workshops, is titled
"War and Peace Protecting the Arts"; the other
entitled "The Triumph", is located near the
entrance of the restaurant, Le Cinq. Both tapestries come from the first half of the 18th century.
The age of Enlightenment shines over this Gallery,
fostering a delightful sense of participation. The
three chandeliers that grace this space were made
in Murano, the famous island of glassmakers next
to Venice. The commodes are copies of a model
from the Louis XIV period by the École Boulle.
This almost Proustian gallery is a pleasant place
to take tea on an Afternoon of a Faun.

OPPOSITE AND BELOW Entrance to the *Le Cinq*
restaurant from the inner Marble Court, where lunches
and light suppers are served on beautiful days.

OPPOSITE, BELOW AND FOLLOWING PAGE

All along the Gallery, one can take time out for some tea, cakes, and a touch of serenity.

THREE STARS AND ALWAYS A PLEASURE

The restaurant *Le Cinq* acquired its three Michelin stars within three years and has quickly become one of the most cherished addresses for Parisian gastronomy. After going through two sets of wrought iron gates, guests arrive in a vast room decorated in tones of gold and gray, like a private salon in a timeless manor. France and England reign over the premises, with two Louis XIV armoires, Louis XVI medallion chairs decorated with gold leaf, and Regency tables in mahogany. The classic French-style drapes made of gray damask with silver highlights are harmonized with shirred voile blinds. The walls are hung with gold and gray fabric, setting off the armchairs upholstered in a gold woven jacquard with embossed pile. The entrance of the restaurant is distinguished with an Aubusson rug and a handsome clock body made in the early 18th century. Two tall Regency mirrors with gilded, carve wood frames reflect the patio of the Marble Court that abuts the restaurant. There are two imposing Regency consoles separating the main room of the restaurant from the second dining room, which serves as the private English salon for parties of eight diners. The paintings that adorn the walls of Le Cinq are by John Singer Sargent and Jan Both, except for two still lifes from the French School of the 18th century. The pearl and white cameos are vintage pieces from the original George V as it was built in 1928, classified by *Bâtiments de France*.

Le Cinq is an encounter between the most subtle culinary tastes — Tart of artichokes and Perigord black truffles or Bresse chicken with lobster George V style *en cocotte lutée* — and the most elegant conviviality: a veritable advanced course in the art of French dining.

OPPOSITE Entrance to the *Le Cinq* restaurant, at the end of the Gallery.

PAGES 44 TO 49 The restaurant dining room, its array of flowers and its delicacies.

IN VINO VERITAS

Over a period of seven years, nearly 50,000 bottles have been collected in the George V wine cellar by Éric Beaumard, restaurant director of Le Cinq and vice-champion in the worldwide competition for the World's Best Sommelier. From the *grands crus* of Bordeaux to rare Chilean wines, as well as selections from Spain and from the Loire valley, the cellar of the George V has become one of the best in Paris. This wine sanctuary merits a tour in its own right, with its walls and vault build with stones from the Chaillot quarry, like those used to build the Arc de Triomphe in the Place de l'Étoile.

As the Director of the George V during the 1970s, André Sonier offered a very good description of the ideal bartender: "It certainly isn't just someone who knows how to mix thirty different cocktails. Anyone can do that if they just buy the right book. The bartender is a facilitator, confessor, and even a psychotherapist for certain patrons. He should immediately understand the type of customer he is dealing with. He needs to recognize if a given person wants to be alone, without speaking to anyone, or if another is seeking to strike up a conversation."

Because the Bar is incontestably the very heart of the hotel, the place where secrets are entrusted or betrayed, the ideal place for meetings, encounters, beginnings and endings. The soft lighting, tables, Havana leather armchairs and Regency pedestal tables are arranged to accommodate intimacy and conviviality, discretion and lively activity at the same time. The chandelier is from the Tisserand workshops located on Paris' famous Rue du Faubourg Saint-Antoine, the neighborhood dedicated to furniture of every kind. On the sycamore bar, flanked by high barstools, you will see an ongoing parade of every type of cocktail in the world. And for those who love reading, an assortment of newspapers and books await in peaceful coexistence around the fireplace.

OPPOSITE Some of the 50,000 bottles secreted away in the hotel wine cellars.

BELOW A cozy spot for a drink among friends.
RIGHT The Barman prepares orders...

ART DU SALON

The "salon" tradition began in the 18th century, a time when intelligent men and women gathered there to discuss politics, morals and religion. Even though such serious topics are not always on the agenda, the salons are as much the life and soul of the Four Seasons George V as ever: The Salon Anglais with its walls lined with important books and portraits of novelists and poets; the Salon Louis XIII, Salon Napoléon and Salon Régence, which are decorated with antique woodwork and adorned with magnificent original Renaissance fireplaces, one of which was transported from Cosne-sur-Loire. The Salon Louis XIII also features an early 18th century Beauvais tapestry that portrays the history of the emperor of China as imagined by artists of the Enlightenment era. The oak woodwork comes from a castle in Normandy.

In the basement, the Salon Auteuil is a reception area where diners enjoy aperitifs before entering the Salon Vendôme, which is decorated with frescoes that represented the most famous Parisian parks. This vast 465 sq. m. salon also serves as a ballroom. These days, there are hardly any truly important fashion shows, prestigious press conferences or significant events that are not held in the Salon Vendôme. As for the Salon Chantilly, it is evocative of the hotel's origins, with its pure *Art Déco* style.

Paul Valéry wrote, "The time of the finished world is starting". The George V Business Center is one of the most modern of its kind in the world, with all of the communications tools needed for maintaining real-time connections to the entire planet. The décor consists of Toile de Jouy wall coverings and mahogany furnishings. Sixteen people at a time can be accommodated with a high-performance private office with telephone, computer and a color laser printer. Although this Business Center is available, each room and suite in the George V is nevertheless equipped with the latest in office productivity and home automation equipment.

OPPOSITE English Salon library.
PAGE 56 Salon Vendôme, also called the Ballroom.
The English Salon.
PAGE 57 Salon Louis XIII.

A HARBOR IN THE HEART
OF PARIS' GOLDEN TRIANGLE

"There is a telephone operator who is exclusively dedicated to monitoring habits. In a way, she serves as the guests' memory. She will remind this one that it's time for his bath, but she may just as soon advise him, if he is sensitive and has so requested, that there are no crimes reported in the daily newspaper and he may open it without fear. There is no better evidence that hotel life is the only kind that truly caters to human fantasy. Lazy, nocturnal, eccentric – those who choose to live in a hotel are first of all guests, and the law, the imperative, is to remain at their disposal without ever displaying any surprise, whether they should request a few grams of radium or an elephant [...]" (Léon-Paul Fargue, *Le Piéton de Paris*).

Whether you are arriving from New York, Tokyo, Dubai, Munich, London or Sidney, your fatigue will dissolve almost instantaneously in the luxurious, cushy tranquility of your room or suite. Warm, light colors of sun and sky, sand and foam, Carrare marble and golden fittings, canopy beds that are sure to inspire your dreams – your are hereby under the protection of the George V and you may safely succumb to luxury, calm and reinvigorating rest.

A statue of his gracious majesty, Britain's George V, which gave the avenue and thereby the hotel its name, reigns before the elevators. But who actually created this palace?

The adventure began in 1924, when the Société d'industrie hôtelière bought a property of 7,081 sq. m., located at the corners of Rue Quentin-Bauchart, Avenue Pierre-1er-de-Serbie and Avenue George V, from the Marquis de La Ferronnays for the sum of 12 million francs, and another lot of 659 sq. m. from the Count de Blacas d'Aupt for 1.5 million francs. In 1926, the architects Constant Lefranc and Georges Wybo submitted their construction drawings for a building with nine stories, with a façade of 25.60 meters on the Avenue George V and 6 meters on the Avenue Pierre-1er-de-Serbie. But the Société d'industrie hôtelière was quickly dissolved and replaced by the Société de l'hôtel George V, which would carry the palace through to its opening. The main shareholders were French banker Alexis Lazarus, American hotelier Joel Hillman and French hotelier André Terrail, the father of Claude Terrail, the late owner and manager of La Tour d'Argent. André Terrail would also be appointed as director of the hotel. Claude Terrail spoke at length of his childhood in the apartment facing the George V: "One day, when my nanny was having a day off, my father allowed me to stay in one of the hotel rooms. At the time, there was an empty lot next to the George V and, along with my friends, we went there to play with our rolling hoops and balls."

The first owner of the George V, American billionaire Joel Hillman, had asked the French architects Lefranc and Wybo to build a hotel that would be in harmony with its times. In compliance with the laws in force in Paris between the two world wars, buildings could not exceed a height of nine floors. The highly streamlined façade in white stone still stands today as a magnificent example of the architectural creativity of eighty years ago, at the height of the *Art Déco* movement. In April 1928, the new George V was completed, and the high society consisting of people in the media, politics and show business welcomed it with resounding applause. Commenting on the inauguration of the palace in May 1928, the American and British press qualified it as "a superb symbol of the modern French style". It should also be noted that the hotel was built on a former quarry that had furnished the stones used for building the Palais de Chaillot.

Between 1928 and 1931, the hotel was expanded. After the purchase in 1930 of 1455 sq. m. of land at the corner of Avenue George V and Avenue Pierre-1er-de-Serbie, a building with furnished apartments was completed in August 1931 to enlarge the hotel. But the worldwide depression following the market crash of 1929 forced the founders of the Société de l'hôtel George V to sell their assets just a few years later to François Dupré, who had negotiated the loan granted by the Princess de Polignac for the purchase of the land and construction of the building. In 1939, François Dupré reigned over a Hotel George V with the area, volume and architecture as they would remain.

Among his many qualities, this man had very decisive tastes and a clear vision of what it takes to create the soul of a palace hotel: luxury, calm, service and beauty. The matter of indulgence was left to the discretion of the guests, their moods and their personal preferences.

Vintage 17th and 18th century Aubusson and Flanders tapestries, Savonnerie carpets, Napoleon III chandeliers, sumptuous Renaissance fireplaces, Louis XVI clocks: nothing was too beautiful to make the George V one of, if not the most, beautiful jewels of the Champs-Élysées quarter. These hundreds of treasures that were carefully set apart from the auction that was held during the temporary closing of the George V in 1997 are now showcased in their original splendor in the galleries and salons of the hotel.

As Léon-Paul Fargue said, "Passenger ships are readily likened to floating hotels. One might also liken hotels to immobilized passenger ships, beginning with the George V, anchored like a sleek and powdered transatlantic luxury liner on the most aristocratic avenue in Paris, which used to be just a patch of countryside with cottages, is now an inlet of luxury and calm. With its fine, almost fragile, walls of stone and marble and succession of flowering gardens and terraces, the George V bears no resemblance to a living machine, a term that was probably invented by old ladies unaccustomed to precise machinery and dwellings that are, at last, comfortable.

The George V also bears no resemblance to the monumental, sorry palaces where luxury is synonymous with boredom. It is just the right hotel for a clientele that has no attachments to the pre-war period, a clientele that is intimately connected with the Jazz age, high-speed living and fluctuating exchange rates, for which the management created a taxi-plane service to pick up the tourists as they arrive on the cruise ships."

The Roaring Twenties. The Depression Era. The triumph of *Art Déco* and *Art Nouveau*. As everyone knows, the worse things became, the more human beings delighted in dancing on the rim of the volcano. The great depression, which as we now know, would lead to catastrophe in ten years, did nothing to prevent the palace on the Avenue George V from enjoying the intense favor, right from the start, of princes and princesses, whether of ancient or recent nobility, financiers, artists, writers or sports celebrities. All the cream of Paris met there.

Right from the start in 1928, they were all on hand. In particular, this included the great Sacha Guitry, who chose it as the scene for his breakup with Yvonne Printemps and his new romance with Jacqueline Delubac. The master's secretary, Fernande Choisel, recounts, "On April 25th, 1932, about twenty of his closest friends met for a meal in a salon at the Hotel George V. Sacha and Yvonne were presiding over a table garnished with flowers. He was celebrating his thirty years in the theater. The highly original menu promised the diners such delicacies as *consommé 'Jacqueline,' salade de 'printemps,' bombe 'illusionniste,'* a *'Madeleine' du théâtre*, and *'eau de la fontaine'* according to the Pasteur system. The conversation was lively; the mood was relaxed – for those who were not in on the secret. Dufrény, Georges Lemaire and I all had aching hearts as we watched. We knew it was probably the last meal they would preside over together. Everything was about to fall apart. Yvonne had tasted a breath of freedom, while Sacha was still wrapped up in his words and taking care of his own circle. He knew that he had the ultimate remedy for suffering: applause. Neither of them was the sort who enjoy torturing themselves by going over every sentimental problem from the beginning. They had made their decision, each one on their own side, without making a last stand." After the split-up, Yvonne Printemps moved in to the George V for a while. As for Sacha Guitry, he used the restaurant and bar of the hotel to try out his most biting repartees, before a delighted audience. One example of his highly cultured pearls: "If somebody steals my wife, the thing that saddens me the most is that he will know what I settled for."

HOTEL   GEORGE V

Salons de Réception

31
AVENUE GEORGE V
PARIS

LA GRANDE SALLE DES FÊTES

OPPOSITE Counts, princesses, and baronesses leaving after the annual Prix de Drags luncheon held at the George V, 1930s.
FOLLOWING PAGE The Gallery and Bar in the 1930s.

Princes and princesses, grand dukes and aristocrats, barons and baronesses and what remained of the royalty in Europe and Asia all took their quarters at the George V. "According to the expression so cherished by the Americans, living in a hotel now seems to be the ideal for many Parisian ladies," wrote the magazine *Paris-Soir* in February of 1935. Now the artist Jeanne Marnac has joined in, leaving her luxurious lodgings on the Avenue Foch for a comfortable apartment in a palace next to the Champs-Élysées, and auctioning off her collections, antique furnishings and art objects. She says, "I am swimmingly happy and carefree." Isn't that what really matters, these days?"

The Princess de Polignac – a shareholder in the company that owned the George V – had her own reserved table, and so did the Maharaja of Kapurthala, who had come from his kingdom in India specifically to enjoy the charms of the City of Light. He insisted that the corridors leading to his suite be adorned with fresh carnations, so they were replaced every day. Another distinctive characteristic of this monarch was his insistence that his dogs should drink only Évian. The Maharaja believed himself to be the reincarnation of Louis XIV and made his courtiers wear wigs and drink red wine. There was no shortage of whimsy! For example, it was unthinkable to attend the Prix des Drags, at the Auteuil race course, or Deauville, without first lunching in the marble court of the palace. In March 1935, the British *Daily Mail* said, "The restaurant at the Hotel George V proves that it is one of the most popular in the French capital, and many well-known personalities are frequently encountered there."

During those years, the management of the palace had the original idea of offering its guests a recorded meal: all conversations were recorded under the table, and when leaving, they could pick up the minutes of the meal along with their coats, in order to build a home library of conversations. Nowadays, the hotel management would get into serious trouble for surveillance of this kind! But at the time, the author Fargue hailed it as an initiative that was "useful for reminding important people that they had promised to take care of you, reminding women that they loved you, and reminding friends that they lied."

Another innovation launched by the George V was the idea of bridge lessons, followed by tea served in the luxurious gallery of the hotel. These weekly bridge teas very quickly brought together all of the upper crust: from Patinos to the Aga Khan, the Princess de Faucigny-Lucinge and the most sought-after and dreaded gossip in the American press, Elsa Maxwell, fascinating in her ugliness. In February 1936, Max Blouet, director of the George V, returning from a six-week tour of the United States, confided in journalists that "American tourism professionals are convinced that this will be the best year for travel to Europe since 1929. It would be even better if people in the United States didn't have the unfortunate idea that Europe is thinking of war. I assured them that people have no bellicose ideas. On the contrary, we are seeking to keep the peace and increase our prosperity." You might say that Blouet didn't exactly have a prophetic gift.

Meanwhile, the palace did everything to assure its guests of the utmost in service, speed and comfort. From April 1937, it began offering transportation by private car between Le Bourget airport and the hotel, and a few months later, for the coronation of

King George VI, the hotel reserved VIP places at Westminster Abbey: they were flown over that morning, provided with a picnic lunch and returned in time for a gala coronation dinner that same evening at the George V. Likewise, American or British tourists landing at Le Havre or Southampton were taken in charge from the moment of their arrival and shuttled by taxi-plane to the airport nearest to the Champs-Élysées. Air taxis linked Paris to London, Berlin and Madrid. Elegant ladies and gentlemen had only to express their wishes, and the George V would take care of everything, including excursions in a three-seater BB Nieuport to play golf in Deauville or Le Touquet. Much later, in October 1970, the world's eight best golfers stayed at the George V for the Tournament of Champions in Saint-Nom-la-Bretèche. Eddy Palmer had his favorite ham flown in from New York for breakfast. But the suite he had been given aroused the envy of his compatriot Floyd, who decided that his apartment was not as opulent and threatened to leave two hours after arriving. Another apartment had to be found immediately, and decorated with a few masterpieces, to convince the champion to stay.

BELOW AND OPPOSITE Luggage, strong boxes
and impeccable linens...

But stars and proto-jet-setters have not been the only ones to grace the George V in its heyday. Politicians have been quick to appreciate the comfort and discretion of this hotel. Thus the famous Young Plan, which sealed Germany's debts to the Allies, was signed in 1931 in the hotel's Salon Bleu, later renamed the Salon Young. Owen D. Young, who stayed in the hotel throughout the conference that concluded with the plan bearing his name left with the chair he had been sitting on during the talks, as well as the green table cover that had adorned the conference table. Upon his return to the United States, he organized a banquet each year to commemorate the event, never failing to sit in his favorite chair. One of the most frequent guests at the time was the mother of President Franklin Delano Roosevelt, who never even considered visiting Paris without staying at the George V. Which inspired Léon-Paul Fargue (clearly – and justifiably – an admirer of the hotel) to comment that the latter "became a part of the complicated history between 1920 and 1935 and will certainly be cited in the books written for secondary education in the 21st century, as a historical monument."

OPPOSITE 2ⁿᵈ French Armored Division tanks during a visit to Paris by Eisenhower, American General and statesman, September 6, 1944.

The year was 1939. Final glimmers before the apocalypse; a cloudless May sky, in June suddenly torn asunder... *Blitzkrieg,* war, occupation. The George V, like all the other Parisian palaces, was requisitioned by the German army and became the headquarters for Marshal Gerd von Rundstedt. The swastika flew over the Champs-Élysées. *Bonjour* to sorrow, shame and horror.

But the bad times would come to an end. On August 26th, 1944, General de Gaulle led a rejoicing crowd down the Champs-Élysées in a liberated Paris. "At three o'clock in the afternoon, I arrived at the Arc de Triomphe [...]. I relit the flame. [...] Before me lay the Champs-Élysées! Ah! The sea! A crowd had gathered from one side of the pavement to the other. Perhaps two million souls. The rooftops were covered with people too. As far as the eye could see, it was a living swell, under the sun, under the tricolor flag." (Charles de Gaulle, *War Memoirs*). Rumor has it that he made a small detour via the Avenue George V to quench his thirst briefly at the bar of the hotel, which was graced once again with the blue, white and red French flag.

The war was over and the Allies settled in at various Paris hotels. General Eisenhower, the hero of the landing on June 6th, 1944, decided to set up the headquarters of SHAPE (Supreme Headquarters Allied Powers Europe) at the George V. He would remain there for 18 months and never failed to visit during subsequent trips to France. According to the hotel employees' recollections, in terms of gastronomy, Eisenhower was mildly maniacal. For example, he would order a turkey, but not the usual kind. He wanted it roasted, but natural, i.e., without any browning, so it would look like it was just plucked. The first time he received the order, the chef nearly panicked. But he thought for a moment and came up with the idea of surrounding the turkey with several layers of aluminum foil, so that it would steam. But the hotel never begrudged this illustrious guest for such caprices. And in January 1953, when Dwight Eisenhower became the President of the United States, he received from the director of the George V a 152-year-old bottle of cognac that had come from the private collection of Napoleon Bonaparte. The George V wanted to offer the general something that money could not buy.

It was truly during this period that the Hotel George V became the Parisian arm of the American movie and theater world. Naturally, Hollywood had not waited for the end of World War II to land in Paris, and in particular at the George V. In 1938, Cécile Sorel held a cocktail reception there in honor of Marlene Dietrich. It was after an encounter at the hotel bar that the divine Marlene fell in love with Jean Gabin and that they began their story of cyclical, tumultuous relations. But starting in the 1950s, the stars were spreading the word: it was only from the terraces of this palace, and nowhere else, that you could enjoy the most beautiful view over Paris. It was in this restaurant, and nowhere else, that you could enjoy lobster with chocolate sauce while rubbing elbows with billionaire Calouste Gulbenkian, actor Burt Lancaster – literally crazy about snails, ordering them with every meal – Katharine Hepburn, Clark Gable, Buster Keaton, Charlie Chaplin, and countless others.

The salons of the George V were then adopted for the fashion shows from Dior, Balenciaga, Schiaparelli and Patou – remember, the Avenue Montaigne is only a few dozen meters away. A maître d'hôtel would discretely whisper to you anecdotes about the famous people of the world, such as oil magnate J. Paul Getty, who made the George V his Paris home, but who was so frugal that once when he received a gift of two magnums of champagne, he asked the bartender if he could pour them into six separate bottles so his guests would not drink it all at once.

Léon-Paul Fargue, once again, said, "The hotel is a country in miniature. People are born, they suffer, they work and sometimes they even die there. Some people choose hotels as the place to commit suicide, because it is a practical place to die. Still others have yet to find anything better to do there than fully enjoy adultery. Some consider a hotel to be a refuge. A hotel is a charming place to stay for those whose hearts are weary of the struggles of life."

And so it was that one day in 1960, they found the wife of filmmaker Henri-Georges Clouzot, Véra, drowned in her bathtub, strangely reminiscent of the movie *Les Diaboliques*. One year earlier, a 16-year-old American named Philip Visson, who had come to spend two months at the George V with his parents, stayed for nearly the whole time shut in the bathroom, where he painted some seventy paintings, which were then shown in a famous *avant-garde* gallery in New York. One of the most subtle novels by Georges Simenon, *Maigret voyage,* begins with a suicide attempt and a murder in two connecting rooms at the George V.

"If Commissioner Maigret had been expecting problems, he wouldn't have expected them to occur at the Hotel George V, which he would have seen as a place that is spoken of more frequently in society columns than in miscellaneous news items. The marble lobby in the George V was deserted, with only the night clerk on one side, who was reading a newspaper behind his mahogany desk, and the concierge on the other side, who was doing nothing." Then Maigret comes to the bar. "There were many personalities that Maigret knew by name: two former kings who had reigned in their own lands and now lived on the Riviera, a former queen who lived in Lausanne, a few princes, an English movie director, the owner of a top brand of whisky, a ballet dancer, a tennis champion..." This novel dates from 1957, but the atmosphere in the bar has not changed, nor the caliber of its patrons.

All of them, whether heads of state, generals, society women or those of other strata, stars and unknowns, converge at some point at the heart of the palace, which is in the bar.

As the central character in this place, the bartender is not only the person who knows how to concoct a hundred different cocktails, he also knows immediately which type of customer he is dealing with. Especially when these customers are pilots as famous and daring as Costes and Bellonte: indeed, it was in the bar at the George V that they made the bet to attempt the first Atlantic crossing, which was, at the time, tantamount to going to the moon. But this did not discourage our two heroes, who later celebrated their achievement in style at the same palace.

An American in Paris? No, it's more like a hundred, a thousand, ten thousand Americans in Paris. Like Gene Kelly, they come to dance on the banks of the Seine, in front of the Eiffel Tower, on the Place de la Concorde, or even more often, in the salons and Ballroom of the George V. In fact, the director of this cult movie, Vincente Minnelli, made it his preferred Parisian residence, and so did his daughter Liza Minnelli, who has not failed to stay here regularly during her Paris visits. The famous producer Darryl Zanuck – Juliette Gréco's companion - occupied an apartment on the 8th floor during the mid-sixties, keeping it for an entire year. A concierge at the George V exclaimed, "Hollywood is what feeds us."

One of the heroes of the late 1960s was neither a star, nor a director or producer, but the writer Albert Cohen, whose masterpiece, *Belle du Seigneur,* had just been published by Gallimard and who also chose to make the George V his Parisian domicile. Another author found himself in the spotlight at almost the same time: dramatist Jean Anouilh, who received the Cino del Duca World Prize in the salons of the George V, in the presence of the finest of Parisian writers, journalists and society. Anouilh exclaimed, "This is the first time I have won a prize and also the first time for me to speak in public. So I am losing my virginity twice today." Later, Chilean author Pablo Neruda chose to stay at the George V during his years of exile. He wrote at least two of his books there, and it was from his favorite hotel that he flew off to Stockholm to receive the Nobel Prize.

Every time something big happens in the capital, French and foreign journalists invade the hotel, whether they are there to interview Federico Fellini, Jack Nicholson, Sophia Loren, Charles Bronson, Robert Redford, Jerry Lewis or one of many other celebrities.

Jerry Lewis made a notable impression on the hotel. One afternoon, in the hotel lobby, some small children were playing while they waited for their parents. Jerry Lewis, who was also waiting to leave, began playing with them, and turned the whole lobby into a gigantic show with his mimics, making everyone in the surroundings laugh so hard they were crying. The hotel staff will always remember this wondrous moment.

Another one who left an unforgettable memory, by his absence, was Orson Welles. Staying in Paris as he filmed *The Trial*, adapted from the novel by Franz Kafka, he reserved a suite at the George V, dropped off his luggage, and disappeared. He only returned to the hotel to retrieve his bags on the day of his departure. A great friend of Welles, the wonderful Jeanne Moreau, shared her moving recollection of the George V. It was in a room of this same hotel that Alfred Hitchcock himself photographed her at great length one afternoon. She recounts, "When I posed for Hitchcock, during the sixties, he said to me, 'I don't film the kitchen sink. So we are going to photograph you in a luxury suite of the George V. I don't want to see you in your kitchen, like everybody else, peeling vegetables." In contrast, this was precisely what Sophia Loren wanted, when she checked into the George V in September 1996 to work on the film *Soleil*, with Philippe Noiret, directed by Roger Hanin. A kitchen was installed in her suite so that her assistant could prepare her favorite pasta.

Different strokes: the king of aviation, Marcel Dassault, would move in with his wife whenever their domestic staff was on holiday. Their only demand was that they be permitted to bring their own bottles of wine.

It was during the same time, in 1969, that Charles Forte, patron of the hotel chain of the same name, became the new owner of the George V; one year later, he appointed a new hotel director, André Sonier, former assistant director of the Carlton in Cannes. This new director dedicated himself to restoring the hotel's status as a temple of celebration, comfort and profitability, a virtue that had apparently been somewhat neglected. He was determined to restore to their rightful places the sculptures of Napoleon by Houdon, the Boulle furnishings and the sumptuous brocades that had been stored away under layers of naphthalene. And, thanks to his friendship with art dealer Paul Pétridès, ten paintings by Maurice Utrillo were hung on the walls of the restaurant *Les Princes*. The George V hosted one of the leading political TV shows, called "Le club de la presse," directed by Jacques Sallebert and Igor Barrère. The "April in Paris" ball was the high point of the year in those days: two hundred American and fifty English guests from New York and London would dance until dawn to the sound of Russian orchestras and rock bands.

André Sonier also sought to restore the image of the George V in another particularly delicate domain: that of unmentionable nighttime pleasures. Indeed, for many years, the basement of the palace housed the Beauty Bar, a very welcoming place that attracted all the women in Paris who were low on virtue and high in expenses. Since the elevator directly linked the basement to the upper floors of the hotel, guests only needed to bring the lady of their choice straight to their rooms, a fact that could implicate the hotel management in prostitution. The legendary hotel seemed to be turning into another kind of establishment. Sonier shut down the Beauty Bar once and for all, and went even further than that: he told the bartender on the ground floor of the hotel not to serve unaccompanied women at all.

OPPOSITE AND BELOW Front of the George V and its Marble Court as decorated in the 1970s.

Which triggered a scandal among feminists. The same thing happened next door, at Le Fouquet's, setting off another wave of indignant protests.

The 1970s were also the time of the *nouveaux riches* from the pop music world. All over the world, young people were rocking to the beat of the Beatles and the Rolling Stones. The latter have chosen to stay at the George V for all of their Paris concerts, even today, and have not failed to awaken neighboring guests with rambunctious parties or all-night jam sessions. Nevertheless, Keith Richards has always written an apologetic note to the hotel director, who carefully preserves them in his records. At times, the fun has disintegrated into hostility. The Stones' drummer, Charlie Watts, was quick to smash the camera of a journalist in the lobby of the George V. But Ray Charles, Cat Stevens and Blood, Sweat and Tears have proven to be calmer guests.

The above shouldn't be taken to mean that the George V is only for American and British stars. French celebrities come here too, on a daily basis, in large numbers, whether Yves Montand or Dalida, crowned with the applause of the music-halls, or others like Michel Audiard, who feels that a hotel room is the best place in Paris to write in peace. When the late, great dialogue author was awarded the French *Légion d'honneur*, there was a memorable dinner held at the George V, during which Lino Ventura and Jean Gabin really cut loose: Gabin, completely uninhibited at two in the morning in the middle of the lobby, delivered his imitation of Raimu in *Les Gaietés de l'escadron*.

RIGHT Prince Alwaleed, owner of the George V since 1996.
Isadore Sharp, founder and CEO of the Four Seasons Group,
ensuring the operation of the George V.
OPPOSITE AND FOLLOWING PAGE The George V under
renovation, Summer 1999.

The years have gone by, along with a succession of owners and directors, each one of which has been unique. While the old George V lived out its final hours, François Mitterrand nevertheless chose it for his first press conference in 1981, the day after his election as President of the Republic.

In the late 1980s and especially in the early 1990s, the George V seemed to drift into a kind of languid routine that could, over time, be dangerous for such a palace where quality, history and beauty have led guests to entertain legitimately high expectations. Occupancy of the hotel was declining and, in 1996, it was put up for sale. It was quickly bought up for 145 million euros by Prince Alwaleed Bin Talal Bin Abdul Aziz Al-Saud, the nephew of King Fahd of Saudi Arabia. When asked why he chose to buy the George V, Alwaleed replies, "Simply because it is the best hotel in the world." He immediately entrusted its management to the Four Seasons group, based in Toronto, which currently administers seventy-one luxury hotels on five continents. Isadore Sharp, founder and CEO of Four Seasons, says that the George V was the most prestigious way for his group to make an entrance into the European scene. Usually, when a grand hotel embarks on necessary renovation work, the owners and managers approach it by transforming one part of the hotel after another, step by step, keeping the hotel open so they will not lose all of their clientele. So this was probably the first time in the history of palace hotels that a radically different approach was taken.

The George V was closed down completely for two years, all personnel were laid off, with all the requisite legal compensation, of course, a portion of the furnishings were sold at auction and the hotel would not reopen its doors until late December 1999. Under the guidance of architect Richard Martinet, all the façades of the hotel as well as the salons and the famous open-air marble court received a thorough face-lift. From floor to ceiling, and including terraces, balconies, windows and stairways, 80,000 sq. km. of paint, 20,000 sq. m. of marble, and 15,000 sq. m. of carpeting were used. The total cost of the project came to 114 million euros.

The Hotel George V of the year 2000 had regained its splendor of old: everything had been redone from top to bottom in order to marry the classic style of the legendary palace with the ultramodern comfort demanded by the globetrotters of the new century. The director of the hotel, Didier Le Calvez, who had refined his skills at the helm of the Plaza in New York, the Regent in Singapore and the Pierre in New York, asserted that the George V needed to be both the most Parisian hotel in Paris and the most international hotel in the world, combining the particular charms of the City of Lights with the highest standards of comfort, quality, service and courtesy that anyone should expect from an establishment of this standing. And he has kept this promise. For the last six years, the George V has regularly been ranked by the most respected travel magazines as the best hotel in the world.

The hotel has two hundred forty-five rooms, of which the smallest has over 35 sq. m. of space. This total number includes fifty-nine suites that range in area from 70 to 380 sq. m., including three presidential suites and two royal suites. There are thirty-six suites with terraces and balconies offering a view over the Eiffel Tower and half of Paris. Pierre-Yves Rochon, who handled all of the interior decoration, restored to their place of honor the fine artworks that adorned the George V from its earliest days, adding about a hundred more pieces that he purchased from antique dealers throughout France. Everything has been

PAGE 88 The English Suite parlor; The Empire Suite parlor.
PAGE 89 The Foyer Chantilly.
OPPOSITE Candlelight dining in the Salon Vendôme.
RIGHT Bouquets by Jeff Leatham, the palace's
veritable signature.

planned to provide a look and feel of comfort and softness: shades of beige, gray and off-white, halogen lamps and soft materials, from the bathrobes to the sheets, curtains and towels. The item that is most in demand at the Four Seasons George V boutique is the king size mattress that guarantees a perfect night's sleep. Anyone who stays in a room or a suite at the George V becomes the king or queen for a day - or night - of their own domain, like a baby in a cradle carefully tended by a host of good fairies.

The nine salons in the hotel have also been completely redone: oak bookcases in the English salon, ornate wood trim and magnificent fireplaces in the Napoleon, Louis XIII and Regency salons, the immense Ballroom and Foyer Vendôme that precedes it, with four paintings - as a nod to the name - representing the four seasons. And to finish, a reference to the hotel's origins, with the Chantilly Salon, completely dedicated to *Art Déco*.

The lobby floor is composed of three types of marble from different origins, while its space leads to the great open-air court that welcomes those who enjoy outdoor lunch or dinner from early spring onward. Like any self-respecting bar in an international grand hotel, the bar is specially appointed to favor the discreet charms of conversation, negotiations, laughter and banter or simply the genuine pleasure of spending some time in a luxurious, soothing, comfortable place.

In the gallery, decorated with tapestries and accented with a background of piano music, light meals and five o'clock tea are served, in the grand tradition of the George V. At the end of the gallery is one of the showpieces of the new Four Seasons George V: the restaurant Le Cinq, graced with splendid bouquets by Jeff Leatham - the veritable signature of the palace, with flower arrangements that require a weekly supply of fifteen thousand flowers! The restaurant offers ample armchairs and tables that are sufficiently isolated to ensure that nothing will disturb any conversations. Here is where Éric Beaumard, restaurant director and Best Sommelier of France, officiates, while Philippe Legendre presides over the cuisine. This chef, who was formerly at the famous Taillevent, had only to cross the Champs-Élysées

BELOW AND OPPOSITE Far from tiresome stress,
the Pool and Spa.

to make Le Cinq into an essential gastronomic landmark. When you go to Le Cinq for lunch or dinner, try to persuade Éric Beaumard or one of his assistants to take you to the basement of the hotel for a tour of one of the most impressive wine cellars in Paris: the walls of this section of the former Chaillot quarry are made of stone like that used to build the Arc de Triomphe at the Étoile. No doubt, the Bordeaux, Burgundy, Alsace or California wines stored here are improving happily in the protective shadow of these legendary stones.

There is another basement area with a completely different ambience: all jet lagged travelers, exhausted e-mailers and worn-out negotiators can get back in shape at the Spa, one of the great new features of the renovated palace. Here, you will not find the drab, neutral tones of a gym, but a Louis XVI décor where you can swim laps in the pool, try out the twelve cardio exercise and body-building machines, tone up your body in the sauna or in a massage room or treat yourself to the joys of aromatherapy. The paintings recreate a forest scene with ferns, the light is filtered, the music is ethereal and you will soon feel reborn, like the Phoenix, leaving behind every trace of fatigue and stress.

PUCCI

It should not be forgotten that the George V is located right in the heart of Paris luxury and history. Between the Champs-Élysées, Avenue George V and Avenue Montaigne, it is a celebration of high fashion, top models, designers and the French art of dressing. From boutiques to fashion shows, and designers to their elegant clients, many come here to see beauty ensconced in creative invention. Dior, Versace, Vuitton, Smalto, Chanel and many more make the immediate environs of the George V into Europe's largest art gallery, where all those who enjoy observing how we dress, and how we mask and unmask one another regularly meet two or three times a year, to celebrate this quest for perfection.

And so it goes, the ongoing spectacle and poetry of the whole range of entertainment that Paris by night can offer its visitors. The guests of the George V may readily go to admire the girls at the Lido or the dream creatures at the Crazy Horse Saloon, relax at Le Fouquet's, attend concerts at the Théâtre des Champs-Élysées or plays at the Théâtre Marigny, go shopping at the *Haute Couture* houses, indulge in gourmet delights at Hédiard, set off on a *bateau-mouche* at the Alma bridge for a lazy excursion along the Seine, or go rub elbows with the Paris "in" crowd at the VIP Room or Mathy's Bar. Excitement is only a few steps away.

CHRISTIAN LACROIX

PAGES 94 TO 97 Some of the luxury boutiques of Paris' Golden Triangle.
FOLLOWING PAGE The George V lights up at dusk, mid 1990s.

BELOW Every morning, each hotel room and suite
is equally inspected (from left to right : Véréna Fox,
Martial Meneghini, Olivier Bihel).
OPPOSITE At *Le Cinq*, it's time for the briefing (from left
to right : Jean-Claude Wietzel, Stéphanie Biondini,
Marc Olivier Raffray).

Feeling a little tired after a good show, dining, dancing and taking in everything your eyes and ears can handle, you return to the Four Seasons Hotel George V where, around the clock, there are almost than six hundred people busily anticipating and satisfying your least desire or most eccentric request. It is a beautiful night, the bed is soft, you can take the time to chat on the telephone, send e-mails or faxes, from your room to anywhere in the world, then, once you have taken care of your obligations, drift off to sleep.

Daybreak. Several silhouettes can be seen on the rooftops, slowly moving on the many terraces of the hotel. The security detail is also at work, twenty-four hours a day, walkie-talkies in hand. Here, every guest can feel as safe and protected as a child.

Alas, the time must always come to say farewell. A steady pace of comings and goings are the fare of the great palace hotels of the world. We have enjoyed some very rich moments at the George V. We will be sure to return as soon as possible. If, as Hemingway said, Paris is a moveable feast, then the George V has become the fireworks, once again.

Paris 1993

En Souvenir
de ma première collection
de Haute Couture, juillet 64
qui se passa dans
les salons du Georges V
un retour nostalgique
avant le passage de
l'ère des poissons à l'ère
du Verseau

amitiés

Paco Rabanne

REGULAR GUESTS AT THE GEORGE V

Fanny Ardant
Rosanna Arquette
Ann Bancroft
The Beatles
Ali Bhutto
Bjorn Borg
Charles Bronson
James Brown
SAR Sultan de Brunei
Claudia Cardinale
Leslie Caron
Jimmy Carter
Ray Charles
Bill Clinton
Georges-Henri Clouzot
Loyd Cole
Gary Cooper
Timothy Dalton
Jim Davis
Marcel Dassault
Alain Delon
Cecil B. DeMille
Vittorio De Sica
Marlène Dietrich
Faye Dunaway
Bob Dylan
Dwight D. Eisenhower
Duke Ellington
Felipe de Borbon
Fischer-Dieskau
Jason David Frank
Pierre Fresnay

Gerald Rudolph Ford
Jean Gabin
Greta Garbo
Vittorio Gassman
Ben Gazzara
J. Paul Getty
Mel Gibson
Hugh Grant
Jerry Hall
Estelle Hallyday
Johnny Hallyday
Roger Hanin
Rex Harrison
Isaac Hayes
Barbara Hendricks
Audrey Hepburn
Charlton Heston
Humbert II d'Italie
William Hurt
Jill Ireland
Jeremy Irons
Michael Jackson
Jean-Michel Jarre
Elton John
Buster Keaton
Gene Kelly
Klaus Kinski
Henry Kissinger
Eartha Kitt
Kevin Kline
Burt Lancaster
Vivien Leigh

Jerry Lewis
Gina Lollobrigida
Sophia Loren
Vanessa Mae
Jane Manson
Lea Massari
Robert Maxwell
John Mellencamp
Sergio Mendes
Michel de Roumanie
Julia Migenes-Johnson
Liza Minelli
Ornella Muti
Olivia Newton-John
Jack Nicholson
Richard M. Nixon
Philippe Noiret
Jessye Norman
Gérard Oury
Helen Paige
George Patton
Paul de Grèce
Luciano Pavarotti
Juan Domingo Peron
Sydney Poitier
Sydney Pollack
Carlo Ponti
Leontyne Price
Yvonne Printemps
Anthony Quinn
Lorenzo Quinn
Charlotte Rampling

Marie-Claire Restout
Dino Risi
The Rolling Stones
Prince Ruspoli
Meg Ryan
Maximilian Schell
Lallo Schiffrin
Helmut Schmidt
Maria Schneider
Omar Sharif
Yves Simon
Dave Stewart
Jacky Stewart
Meryl Streep
Donna Summer
Chantal Thomass
Gene Tierney
Charles Trénet
Pierre Trudeau
Tina Turner
Victor-Emmanuel
de Savoie
Roch Voisine
Charlie Watts
John Wayne
Raquel Welch
Orson Welles
Barry White
Tony Joe White
The Who's
Terence Young
Michaël York

THE ROYAL TREATMENT

The George V has 59 suites, including two royal suites and three presidential suites, four thematic suites and three two-level suites. The largest suites feature an equipped kitchen and dining room for eight to ten. The 18th and 19th century paintings hang alongside contemporary works, while the clocks are from the Restoration period and the middle of the 19th century. The well-lighted desks are equipped to let everyone stay connected with the outside world. Most of the beds are large, some are canopied, and the bathrooms are done entirely in marble. Many suites have terraces and balconies that offer some of the finest views possible over the rooftops, church spires and monuments of the neighboring areas of Paris, up to the pyramidal tower designed by Gustave Eiffel.

The Honeymoon Suite is the perfect setting for a marriage made in heaven, with four terraces overlooking the Panthéon, the Invalides, Notre Dame, the Opéra and, of course, the famous Eiffel Tower. The furnishings in this suite are a mixture of 18th century and Renaissance styles. The canopy over the bed and the comforter cover are printed in the Toile de Jouy style, an invitation to luxury, calm and sovereignty. The Empire Suite, a magnificent homage to Napoleon, includes a handsome Egyptian-influenced desk. The French Suite is decorated in the Louis XVI style, with paintings from the French schools of the 19th century. The English Suite is furnished entirely in the romantic style of the 18th century.

OPPOSITE Honeymoon Suite bedroom.
PAGE 112 The parlor in one of the presidential suites. Bedroom in one of the Four Seasons Suites.
PAGE 113 Honeymoon Suite parlor. Bedroom in one of the presidential suites.

OPPOSITE Empire Suite.
BELOW Royal Suite with its Louis XIV desk.

BELOW English Suite bedroom.

OPPOSITE Bathroom in one of the presidential suites.

PAGES 120-121 Honeymoon Suite terrace.

PARADISE ON EARTH

A twenty-five hour flight? Repetitive jet lag? Fatigue and stress? The Spa is on hand to set everything right. There is a swimming pool, sauna, steam bath, relaxation and massage room and, above all, a fitness club equipped with every possible or imaginable machine for cardio routines and weight lifting, in a joyful, rhythmic musical ambience combined with TV screens that bring you every channel broadcasting anywhere on the planet. The décor adds the timeless touch needed in such an upscale establishment: a restored fountain in Burgundy burnt stone and, on the pool's horizon, a *trompe l'oeil* fresco representing the gardens of the Grand Trianon at the Château de Versailles.

Here is where even the most overworked executives can be transformed into devotees in pursuit of a soothing, peaceful, fragrant nirvana. Filtered lighting and warm tones in the décor help make the Spa into something approaching paradise on earth.

PAGES 122 TO 129 The Spa and Pool, a soothing nirvana...
PAGES 130-131 Aromatherapy and body massages
for complete relaxation.

SAY IT WITH FLOWERS!

The sumptuous floral arrangements at the Four Seasons Hotel George V, signed by Jeff Leatham, are an integral part of the hotel's décor and atmosphere. With a team of seven assistants, Leatham devises a new theme each week, refreshing and embellishing his floral sculptures every day, and sometimes every hour. These impressive, ubiquitous compositions add a contemporary touch to the classic setting of this palace.

Every week, about 15,000 flowers are sent from Holland. The floral designer uses them to create ten main arrangements for the lobby and the public areas. Then there are 150 smaller bouquets that decorate the tables, consoles and secretaries throughout the hotel. There are specific arrangements for every room or suite, while a single flower or branch of foliage will add a note of color to the marble bathrooms.

PAGES 132 TO 137 Each week, the palace receives
a resolutely contemporary touch with 15,000 flowers
ordered and arranged by Jeff Leatham.

PAGES 138 TO 141 A play of white for luxury and modernity during the end of year festivities.

PORTRAITS
SELECTED

Éric Beaumard

Originally from Britanny, Éric Beaumard developed his interest for cooking in 1978. After a learning period where he demonstrated his exceptional level of motivation, he began as an apprentice chef in various restaurants until 1981.

In 1982, events turned his career in a new direction. A motorcycle accident slowed him down by depriving him of the use of his right arm. In 1984, following many months of convalescence, he was back on track in his cooking career, with the Maisons de Bricourt in Cancale. There, he held the position of chef for a period of six months. At the urging and advice of Olivier Roellinger, he turned towards wine and the profession of sommelier, and a new calling and a new talent were born.

From 1984 to 1987, Mr. Beaumard worked as the sommelier in a variety of establishments, while continuing his devoted study of the art of wine, successfully participating in a number of sommelier competitions. The title of Best Young Sommelier of France in 1987 earned him a position with the two-star restaurant La Poularde, in Montrond-les-Bains, in the Loire region. In 1992 and again in 1994, he was named as the Best Sommelier of France. In 1998, he finished as vice-champion in the competition for World's Best Sommelier. And in 2003, the magazine *Le Chef* named him as the Best Sommelier of the Year.

Since 2000, Éric Beaumard has been the director of the restaurant Le Cinq, which was awarded the distinction of three stars in the Michelin Red Guide in 2003.

Thierry Hamon

Thierry Hamon is only 31, yet he is already a confirmed grand sommelier, after having trained at La Poularde, one of the gastronomic high points of France and of Navarre (two stars in the Michelin Guide). Mr. Hamon is one of a long and distinguished line of selective, expert tasters who are fully dedicated to wine. As the head sommelier since 2006, he watches over some 50,000 bottles that are laid up in the magnificent wine cellar of the George V. From Petrus to good Chilean or California wines, the fruits of the vine hold no mysteries for Thierry Hamon and his team.

Fabrice Lecleir

Fabrice Lecleir, 33, is the pastry king at the George V. As a hotel pastry cook since 1992, he worked as the pastry chef at the Sofitel Paris La Défense in 2000, before joining the George V in April 2001. That is when he began working together with Arnaud de Faletans to create the desserts for the restaurant Le Cinq. Promoted to the position of pastry chef in July 2004, Mr. Lecleir heads a team of a twelve people who excel at creating refined gourmet delights: *Millefeuille* pastry, Creamy chocolate cake, etc.

But this taste enchanter does not only work in the famous three-star restaurant. You can also savor his cakes, ice creams and *pièces montées* in the Gallery or at the Bar, or during one of the banquets organized by the hotel, and even as far away as New York or Japan, as a part of customary international gastronomic exchanges.

Jeff Leatham

Leatham's creations, whether they are majestic bouquets of lilies in a monumental vase, or a layer of roses floating in a cube of colored glass, always have a decisively modern spirit and stylized shapes that set off the furnishings and colors used in the George V. From the lobby to Le Cinq, the hotel's elegant restaurant, these flower arrangements recall the warm tones of the early 18th century Flanders tapestries that adorn the walls. White, cream and deep-toned color combinations that are often used stand out in sharp contrast against the interior decoration. For private dinners, the tables are graced with a harmonious mixture of the beautiful purity of the flowers and the glimmering lights of a host of candles.

Jeff Leatham is famed for his talent all over the world. He was in charge of the floral decorations for the opening night of the San Francisco Opera, for example, and he participated in the Emmanuel Ungaro *Haute Couture* fashion shows.

Leah Marshall

Leah Marshall is the Canadian contribution to the dynamic energy of the Four Seasons Hotel George V. With a degree from the University of California at Los Angeles, Ms. Marshall began working in the Hospitality department of the Westin hotel in Montréal, then pursued her career within the same chain at various hotels in California, as well as at a number of Disney establishments. After serving as the Director of the Newporter Resort, in California, Ms. Marshall joined the Four Seasons Hotel George V in Paris, where she became the executive *gouvernante* in 1999, then in October 2001, the Director of Hospitality. This is a strategic position, calling for diplomacy, skill and foresight – all feminine qualities – to make sure that no guests feel dissatisfied with their rooms or suites, etc.

Jean-Pierre Soutric
Caroline Mennetrier

In November 1997, Jean-Pierre Soutric joined the staff of the George V as the marketing manager - two years before the hotel reopened. This means he was closely involved with all the details of the renovation, as a true connoisseur of the rules of hospitality that must govern any authentic international palace hotel.

For twenty years, Mr. Soutric has held positions of responsibility in such well-known hotel chains as Hilton International, InterContinental Hotels and Resorts. Before joining the Four Seasons company, he spent two years working as the regional sales and marketing manager at the Forte Paris company, placing his talents at the service of the Plaza Athénée, the Hôtel de la Trémoille and even the George V, which gave him in-depth knowledge about the history and traditions of this establishment. His strong interest in architecture, history and music naturally led him to take a keen interest in every minute detail of all the treasures found in the salons, suites and rooms of the George V.

Having joined the Four Seasons Hotel George V team in 2000, Caroline Mennetrier was appointed Public Relations Director in 2004. Nothing happens at the George V without the knowledge of she who, like Ariadne's thread, guides the world's media along the palace's labyrinths, where every room, suite, and salon contains a Holy Grail...

Our heartfelt thanks to Didier Le Calvez and his management team—Jean-Claude Wietzel, Leah Marshall, Sylvie Rolland, Michel Lefèvre, Marc Olivier Raffray and Jean-Pierre Soutric—, as well as to Jackie Dalena, his personal assistant, and all the staff at the George V.

PHOTOGRAPHIC CREDITS
© Four Seasons Hotel George V/Jaime Ardiles-Arce: p. 28-29, 32-33, 38-39, 44-45, 54-55, 56 (u. and d.), 57, 88 (u. and d.), 89, 90, 110-117, 122-123, 128-131
© Four Seasons Hotel George V/David Arráez: p. 19, 24-25, 27, 30, 34-37, 42-43, 48-52, 91-93, 102-103, 108, 118-121, 124-127, 132-133, 135-141, 148, 156-159
© Four Seasons Hotel George V/Lucien Chauffard: p. 72 (l.)
© Four Seasons Hotel George V/Pierre-Yves Rochon: p. 22, 23
© Four Seasons Hotel George V/Studio Chevolon: p. 58-59
© Four Seasons Hotel George V/DR: p. 4-5, 8, 18, 20-21, 26, 40-41, 53, 60, 64-65, 67, 70, 71, 72 (r.), 73, 78, 82 (u. and d.), 83, 84 (l. and r.), 85-87, 98-99, 104-107
© Jean-Marie del Moral: cover, p. 16-17, 31, 46, 47, 134
© Jean-Marie Francius: p. 144, 152
© Jeremie Bouillon: p. 100, 101, 146, 150, 154
© Lipnitzki/Roger-Viollet: p. 80 (l.)
© ND/Roger-Viollet: p. 10-11, 13 (u. and d.)
© Noa/Roger-Viollet: p. 80 (r.)
© Roger-Viollet: p. 74, 76, 77

Printed in December 2006
by Kapp-Lahure (France)
ISBN: 978-2-7324-3568-6